Giant Pacific Octopus

The World's Largest Octopus

by Leon Gray

Consultant: David Scheel
Professor of Marine Biology, Alaska Pacific University

BEARPORT PUBLISHING

New York, New York

Credits

Cover, © Brandon Cole/brandoncole.com; TOC, © Fred Bavendam/FLPA; 4–5, © Boris Pamikov/Shutterstock; 6, 8, © Brandon Cole/brandoncole.com; 9, © Fred Bavendam/FLPA; 10, © Zach Zartler; 11, 12, © Brandon Cole/brandoncole.com; 13, © Fred Bavendam/FLPA; 14–15, © Brandon Cole/Corbis; 16, R. N. Lee/NOAA; 17, 18, 19, © Fred Bavendam/FLPA; 20, © Ed Lines/Shedd Aquarium; 21, © Brandon Cole/brandoncole.com; 22L, © Eric Cheng; 22C, © Vittorio Bruno/Shutterstock; 22R © Dr. Dirk Schories; 23TL, © Mircea Bezergheanu/Shutterstock; 23TR, © Brandon Cole/brandoncole.com; 23BL, © Boris Pamikov/Shutterstock; 23BR, © R. N. Lee/NOAA.

Publisher: Kenn Goin
Senior Editor: Joyce Tavolacci
Creative Director: Spencer Brinker
Photo Researcher: Calcium Creative

Library of Congress Cataloging-in-Publication Data

Gray, Leon, 1974-
  Giant Pacific octopus : the world's largest octopus / by Leon Gray.
    pages cm. — (Even more supersized!)
  Audience: 6-9
  Includes bibliographical references and index.
  ISBN 978-1-61772-730-6 (library binding) — ISBN 1-61772-730-X (library binding)
  1. Octopuses—Pacific Area—Juvenile literature. I. Title.

  QL430.3.O2G73 2013
  594.56—dc23
                    2012033706

For more information, write to Bearport Publishing Company, Inc., 45 West 21st Street, Suite 3B, New York, New York 10010. Printed in the United States of America.

10 9 8 7 6 5 4 3 2 1

Contents

Ocean Giant

The giant Pacific octopus is the world's largest octopus.

This ocean giant has eight arms.

Each arm can grow up to 16 feet (4.9 m) long.

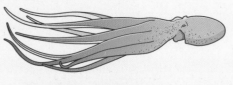

With its arms stretched out, the octopus is about as long as a minivan.

A large male giant Pacific octopus can weigh more than 100 pounds (45 kg). One of the largest ever caught weighed more than 400 pounds (181 kg).

A Watery World

The giant Pacific octopus lives in the Pacific Ocean.

It usually lives in shallow water near the coast.

Yet it may also live in water that is up to 5,000 feet (1,524 m) deep.

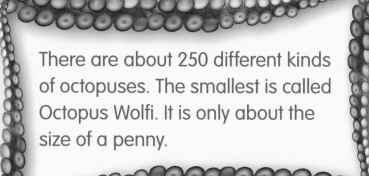

There are about 250 different kinds of octopuses. The smallest is called Octopus Wolfi. It is only about the size of a penny.

Giant Pacific Octopuses in the Wild

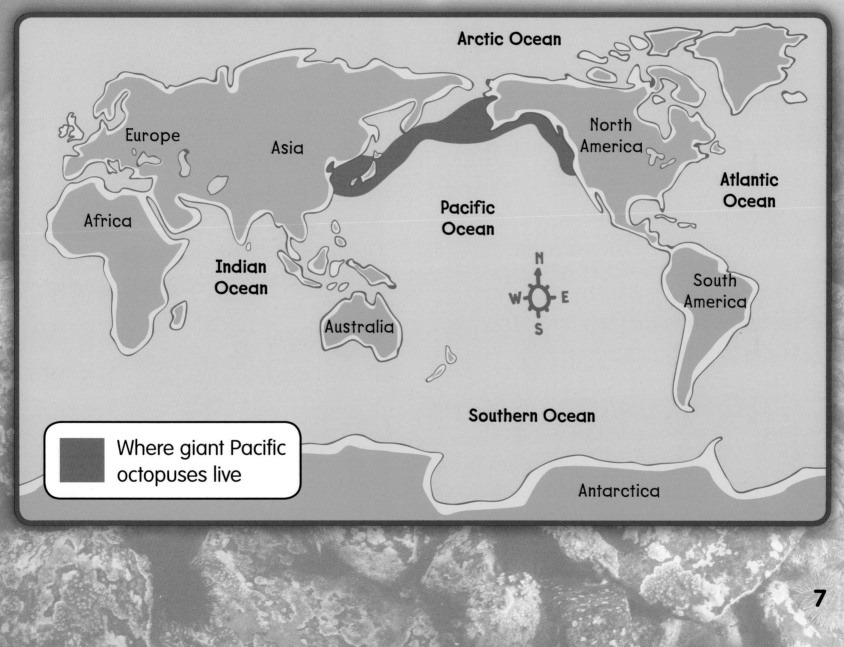

Arctic Ocean

Europe

Asia

North
America

Atlantic
Ocean

Africa

Pacific
Ocean

Indian
Ocean

N
W E
S

South
America

Australia

Southern Ocean

Where giant Pacific
octopuses live

Antarctica

Odd Bodies

The giant Pacific octopus is an odd-looking animal.

Its eight long arms are attached to its head.

Above the octopus's head is a body part called the **mantle**.

Shaped like a sack, the mantle contains the stomach and other important body parts.

The giant Pacific octopus has two rows of up to 280 suckers on each arm. The suckers help the octopus feel and grab on to rocks, as well as taste food.

arm

suckers

Tiny Dens

Like all octopuses, the giant Pacific octopus does not have any bones in its body.

As a result, it can squeeze into small holes or cracks in underwater rocks.

The giant Pacific octopus uses these small, rocky places as its home, or den.

When resting, the octopus hides in its den.

The only hard part of an octopus's body is its beak, which is found at the bottom of its body, in its mouth.

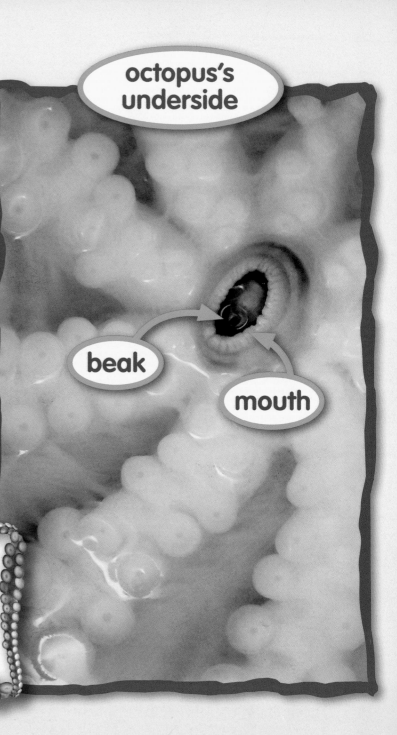

octopus's underside

beak

mouth

10

Dinner!

When it is hungry, the giant Pacific octopus leaves its den to hunt for food.

Crabs, clams, and other animals with hard shells are a few of its favorite foods.

The octopus uses its strong beak to bite open its victim's shell.

With its bite, the octopus also sends poison into its victim to make it stop moving.

After that, the octopus brings the meal back to its den to eat it.

midden

After it has eaten, the octopus pushes any empty shells out of its den. The pile of shells is known as a **midden** or an "octopus's garden."

crabs

Changing Color

The giant Pacific octopus is hunted by many animals.

Seals, sea otters, and whales are just a few of the animals that will kill and eat it.

Luckily, the octopus has a way of hiding from its enemies, even after leaving its den.

It can quickly change its body color in order to blend in with its surroundings.

The giant Pacific octopus can change the look and feel of its skin to help it hide in the ocean. For example, it can make its skin appear smooth or bumpy.

An Inky Getaway

Sometimes, a giant Pacific octopus is spotted by an enemy.

When this happens, the octopus can play another trick with color.

It squirts a cloud of black ink out of its body.

The dark cloud makes it hard for the octopus's attacker to see it.

Meanwhile, the octopus has enough time to escape!

siphon

An octopus can move quickly by pumping water out of a tube-shaped body part called a **siphon**. The octopus sucks in water to fill the mantle and then pushes the water out to shoot itself forward.

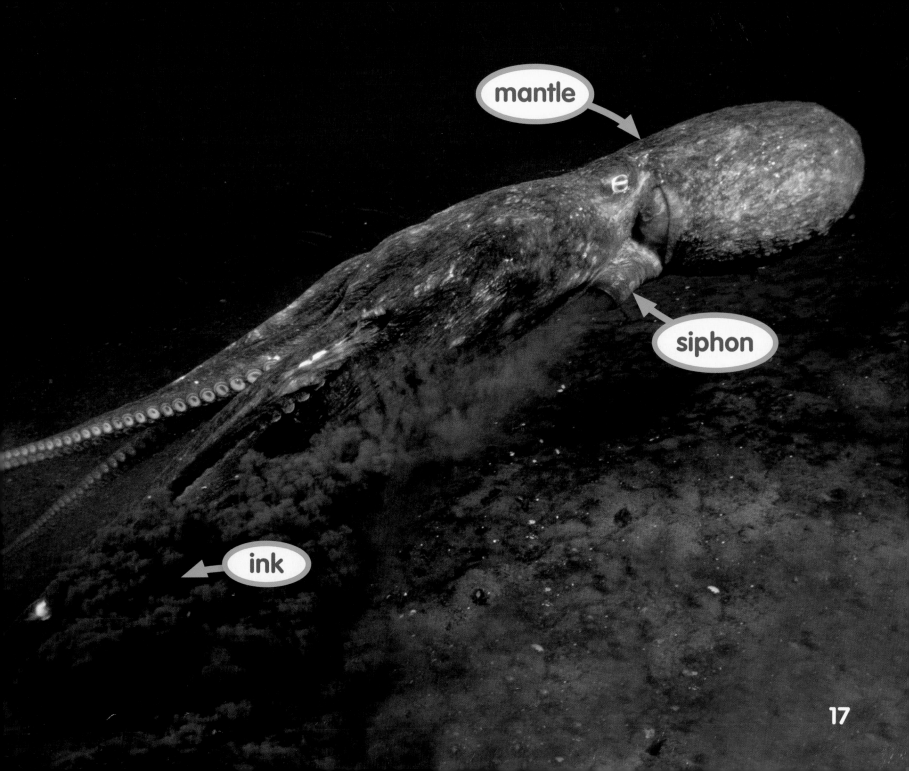

mantle

siphon

ink

From Eggs to Adults

Female octopuses lay up to 75,000 eggs in their underwater dens.

The mothers hang the eggs in strings from the ceilings.

Then they watch over them until they hatch.

When the babies come out, they are tiny.

It will take three years for the baby octopuses to grow to full size.

eggs

baby octopus

Only one or two out of every 50,000 baby octopuses live to become adults. The rest are eaten by other animals.

19

Big and Smart

Because giant Pacific octopuses hide a lot, it is hard for scientists to study them.

At **aquariums**, however, scientists can watch them up close.

They have seen the animals learn new tasks and solve puzzles.

These sea creatures are not just big and shy, they are also smart and curious!

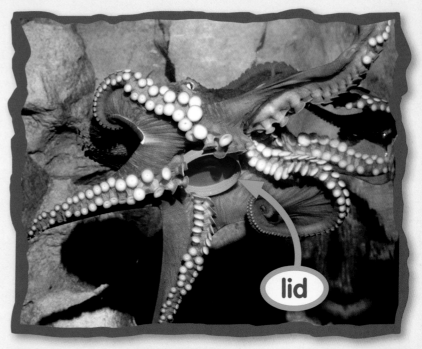

lid

Some giant Pacific octopuses have learned to twist the lids off jars in order to get food that has been placed inside.

More Large Octopuses

The giant Pacific octopus is a mollusk. Mollusks are a group of animals that have a soft body, no bones, and often a hard shell. Mollusks include squids, snails, and clams. Unlike most mollusks, the giant Pacific octopus does not have a shell to protect its soft body.

Here are three more large octopuses.

Seven-Arm Octopus

This octopus is known as the seven-arm octopus because the males curl one of their eight arms up. The octopus can grow up to 6.5 feet (2 m) long.

Common Octopus

The common octopus can grow up to 4.3 feet (1.3 m) long and weigh up to 22 pounds (10 kg).

Southern Red Octopus

The southern red octopus can grow up to 3.3 feet (1 m) long and weigh up to 8 pounds (3.6 kg).

Giant Pacific Octopus
16 feet/4.9 m

Seven-Arm Octopus
6.5 feet/2 m

Common Octopus
4.3 feet/1.3 m

Southern Red Octopus
3.3 feet/1 m

Glossary

aquariums
(uh-KWAIR-ee-uhms)
buildings with large
tanks or pools
where different
kinds of water
animals are kept

midden
(MID-uhn) a
pile of shells an
octopus has left
outside its den

mantle
(MAN-tuhl)
the large, round
section of the
octopus's body that
contains its stomach
and other important
body parts

siphon
(SYE-fuhn)
a tube-shaped
part of an
octopus's body
used to push
out water

Index

Read More

Lindeen, Carol K. *Octopuses (Pebble Plus: Under The Sea).* Mankato, MN: Capstone (2005).

Spilsbury, Louise. *Octopus (A Day in the Life: Sea Animals).* Chicago: Heinemann (2011).

Spirn, Michele. *Octopuses (Smart Animals).* New York: Bearport (2007).

Learn More Online

To learn more about the giant Pacific octopus, visit:
www.bearportpublishing.com/EvenMoreSuperSized